FOR THE MOMENT

Also by John Mole

Poetry

The Love Horse
A Partial Light
Our Ship
From the House Opposite
Feeding the Lake
In and Out of the Apple
Homing
Depending on the Light
Selected Poems

For children

Once There Were Dragons
Boo to a Goose
The Mad Parrot's Countdown
Catching the Spider
The Conjuror's Rabbit
Back by Midnight
Hot Air
Copy Cat
The Dummy's Dilemma

Criticism

Passing Judgements

FOR THE MOMENT
John Mole

PETERLOO POETS

First published in 2000
by Peterloo Poets
The Old Chapel, Sand Lane, Calstock, Cornwall PL18 9QX, U.K.

A catalogue record for this book is available
from the British Library

ISBN 1-871471-82-6

Printed in Great Britain by
Antony Rowe Ltd, Chippenham, Wilts.

ACKNOWLEDGEMENTS

Acknowledgements are made to the following
publications in which some of these poems first appeared:

*Agenda, The Critical Survey, The David Jones Journal,
The Interpreter's House, London Magazine, New
Statesman and Society, Poetry Review, Poetry Wales,
The Rialto, The Shop, Sunday Times, The Spectator,
The Swansea Review, The Times, The Times Literary
Supplement.*

The author would like to thank the Master and Fellows of
Magdalene College Cambridge for their hospitality during
his period as Poet-in-Residence when some of these
poems were written.

To the memory of my mother –
Lilian Joyce

Contents

page

When did you start writing poetry?

When women played boys on the radio
which was wireless, and yo ho ho
roared the pirates with a bottle of rum
over rough waves to Hilversum,

when soap was a special agent
at a quarter to seven, and the traffic went
mightily round Eros with its freight
of film stars, pundits and heads of state,

when a song in the heart was two-way
family favourites, and the Sunday
joint served up with studio laughter's
trimmings meant tinned fruit for afters,

when choice was whatever a housewife
fancied as she wiped the buttery knife
he'd left in the marmalade, and the morning
service passed by with a prayer on the wing,

when the news spoke perfect English
in a teacher's voice, and the dish
ran off with the spoon, and God was there
to say *Good night children everywhere,*

when father came home on the dot
and his tea was ready, and whatever the pot
called the kettle was a secret vice
one never broadcast on the home service,

oh then it began to seem good sense
to turn down the volume, to search for a silence
that nobody but myself could hear,
and to lend to the rest only half an ear.

The War

It stopped when I was four, and everyone
was very happy. We had lemonade and little flags
and jelly, and the wireless gave up on the enemy

and sounded better. Then the Americans went home
to jitterbug, whatever that was, which sounded
just the job, and Mr. Churchill kept on saying

what we owed them in his special growling voice
which Grandad said was bulldog. How to peel bananas
wasn't difficult. You started at the end

then stripped them back. The skin fell past your wrist
and dangled. This was easier than oranges
although I still liked oranges the best, and apples

which were English – Cox's, Worcesters, Ribston Pippins
with their shiny names. So everything was apple pie
and what the doctor ordered. Everything

except my aunt's room where I heard her crying
so I just walked in. She stopped. The bottom drawer
was half-way open. *Look*, she said, and handed me

a little silver strip she'd picked up from her nightdress,
do you know what this is? Then she peeled it
and the silver fell away. *You never met him. This*

is what you do. She put it in her mouth, pale pink,
a second tongue, and chewed, then pulled
and pulled, and out it came all string like conjuring

and looped down almost to the floor until she
sort of skipping-roped it back. *You try,*
she said, *I've got another piece where that came from*

and found it in the drawer. *We used to bet*
on who could make it longest. Which is what we did,
nephew and aunt, there in her room. The war

was over. Everyone was happy, almost,
and the jitterbug still sounded just the job
and I knew somebody who'd teach me how to dance it.

Mr. Harrison

The cut was 1/9,
price of a back seat
at the Gaumont
or just under
three bottles of Corona.

His clippers smelt
of previous hair
and tweaked my
neck and mowed
around each ear.

The comb snagged
everywhere it could,
its greasy teeth
bit to my scalp, the scissors
flat against them, squeaking.

He lit up before
the Brylcream, crowned me
with a dollop, shaped
my duck's-arse
while he coughed.

The ash bent from
a fag-stump
bobbing on his
lower lip, his
slit eyes watered.

The mirror
framed our portrait
in its flaking gilt
where eyes met
and approved his handiwork.

My own gaze
straight ahead, his
angled down, up, side
to side, and then a final
laying on of hands

before the basin's
altar, cut-throat folded
between taps,
a wet brush
stained to yellow.

A shaking
to the floor, a flap
of stiff white sheet,
a breath of nicotine
and oil, and

me beside him,
sudden, tall, triumphant
like an unwrapped
present to myself,
a revelation.

1/9 at Mr. Harrison's
then out his ringing
door past Denis Compton
and the weekend something
blushing on its shelf

The Cigarette

I was our sixth-form writer,
knew exactly how to look in paperback
before I'd typed a word, which meant
tough novels and essentially
the cigarette. The way to hold it
was like this, to prop yourself above
a portable Olympia, your fingers stained
and raking upwards from the palm
which cupped your brow, and that
was how you waited for the inspiration.
There, from the plunging apex of a V,
it stuck out with its brittle droop of ash
about to fall, but you were miles away
in Monterey or Little Rock because
it had to be America, remembering
the hard road to success, the guys
you'd left behind you in the flophouse
and the loneliness of night drives
in the cabin of a twelve-wheel truck.
Then later came the second take
when you had won the Pulitzer,
when naked to the waist, medallioned,
in white bermudas with the cigarette
still smoking at the far tip of your grin,
you faced the *Newsweek* cameras
but with the virtue now gone out of you,
a ghost, an ectoplasmic gauze
around the blur of indecipherable eyes.
And that was how I pictured it, the famous
end to the career I dreamed of
and the price of fame, burnt out,
with every title selling millions
and no need of a photograph at all
except the blown-up still life on each cover
of a last stub lying in its tray.

Summer Afternoon

Voices from the dark square
of an upper window, somewhere
deep inside, invisible beauty
dancing on a quilted bed. How many
and what laughter? As I guessed
the quiet one was the loveliest
but would she step across the floor
to look down on the street? My car
was waiting merely for a friend
and not impatient. Hang around
like this, what else, the radio on
to catch the Beach Boys song
which caught her too. I wasn't wrong.

The Trick

Strap-hanging, shoulder
to shoulder, the trick
was to turn a page
of the *Standard*
pressed to your face
one-handed
and, myopic
as James Joyce,
imagine yourself
in Paris with the girl
who might have
read your horoscope,
who gently leant
against you,
opening her book.

Breakfast at Drumcliff

Summer 1960, Peter and me, drenched by a leaking tent
across the road from Yeats' grave. It had rained all night
and blustered in the dark, but now from the blessed
unzipped fetor of our sleeping bags we rose to breakfast
in an aftermath of sunlight. We had not passed by.

Nor had the Mini blown away. Standing on flattened
shining grass, a snub-nosed Pegasus, its rinsed
metallic flanks prepared to carry us to Ballylee
on wings of song, two would-be student princes
hungry for association with the purple glow.

Last night had clouded over, yes, but not before
Ben Bulben's silhouette had loomed through
thunderous dazzle and the headstone worked
its rhetoric. Something complete, intended,
in its quattrocento posture for the camera's cold eye.

Now, though, breakfast. Back to bundled incoherence,
fumbling the matches, hiss of camping gaz
beneath a battered kettle, rag and bone
of a collapsing tent behind us, and the world
of so much late romantic poetry lying all before.

Simple

(To Charles Causley)

Walking in thin rain by Plymouth harbour,
stopped by a schoolgirl with her questionnaire
and pale attendant Mum. You were all courtesy
while I, superfluous, had nothing I could say
about the latest city plans and must have shown it,
hanging around a few damp yards behind

then coming up again to join you
when they'd done. You said *It's just as well
you waited. Usually if anybody asks me questions
in the street and I'm with someone
younger like yourself, I say
'It's no use asking the boy, he's simple.'*

Oh simple, simple. As we walked together,
me in my shin-length pouchy mac, yes I remembered
simple and the village shape it took, recalled poor moonface Tony
buttoned in his shiny Sunday only suit and hurling
down the aisle without embarrassment
his goatish bleat, or holding out his small change
to be counted for him by the butcher, scuffing the sawdust,
shuffling out to join his train of dogs and children. *There,*
my mother told me, *but for the grace of God
goes every one of us,* and nodded as we passed him
looking sideways, glancing down. I remembered too
my bedside catechism mouthed on pious little knees
Oh pity my simplicity ...

So keep it simple. Wasn't that the way?
Those admonitions, simple acts of kindness,
simple honesty, and Simon in his old rhyme
simplest of all ...

Whatever simple is or was
seemed for a while much more or less than simple
in the shadows of my laughter
at the idiot accomplice you had made me
and that Plymouth harbour wall.

The Cookham Resurrection

A boatload of the resurrected
trailing amazement,
cast off, second-chancing
from a Berkshire village.

See how hesitantly
they renew acquaintance,
dipping earth-stained fingers
in the holy Thames.

Then home to homeliness,
a step up from the tow-path,
sure of their ground
and all they left behind.

To resume in the rinsed
clarity of vision what before
seemed daily, good bread
risen to angel food.

Going once more about
their business, love's
transfiguration of each trade
or sturdy labour

in a field of praise
contiguous with heaven
where the gate stands open
and they pass between.

The King's Astrologers

They stood there, all of them,
and pointed at the sky
as if accusing it
of some great mischief.

Nothing like this
had ever dared to happen,
no such treason
since the world began.

Whatever it meant
was certain danger,
rivers running blood,
a change of heart,

and even as they watched
a star was added
to the constellation
of their ancient cloaks.

A Diptych for David Jones

1.
Wherever he looks with that long gaze inward
is Langland's field full of folk
on a cloth of gold, the numinous Imperium.

What he sees through the sights of a rifle
threads his line to a soldier's tunic
diced for in bloody shame at Mametz Wood.

So many men so beautiful, the albatross's
hung-down Roman head of accusation
still can bless the unaware in all of them

while Bardolph, Lewis, Quilter and John Ball
sail on together through a needle's eye
to rest in glory, grounded under the oak.

2.
Wake the sleeping lord before reveille,
strike a lucifer, its brief flame
mortal as daybreak burnishing his face.

The dew is manna and his soul's ascension
as it steals a march on gravity
to leave earth's greatcoat royally cast aside.

Love, the password between stations,
crosses its heart, forgives the wounded tree
two thousand years have carved their names on

where a ghostly blossom is the snowfall,
flake by flake, of angels' joinery
along its branches, immanently white.

The Green Man

comes home from market,
the rootless tree
in its hair-net
slung like a rifle
over his shoulder.

About his neck
a holly wreath
numbers its berries,
his warm breath
is a garland of air.

In his pockets
the crisp leaves
of next year's diary,
burnished hazelnuts
and a last coin.

Soon the children
with their apple faces
will be dancing round him,
hungry, open-handed
for the season's gifts.

The Erl-King's Daughter

(For Alistair Jolly)

I wanted him, the boy-child snug there
in his father's cloak, the two of them
out riding later than they should
and laughing *What shall we tell your mother?*
as their horse, the little dobbin,
pricked its ears up prettily, *It's past
your bedtime and she warned us
not to come this way.* Oh how the full moon
lit their small adventure, wrapped it cosily
in skeins of innocence, and oh
I had never known such longing ever,
such an illicit midnight fever
draining me, the damp mist
moistening their furs to diamond tips
like everything I'd dreamed of
that my father could not give although
he loved me. *Father,* I said, not loud
because he stood beside me as he always did,
a shadow darker than his shadow,
*call to the child and turn that shining face
towards me. Yours is the voice
that only he will hear, a rustling in the leaves,
a willow whisper, nursery sounds
of cold enchantment.* So he called
and instantly I knew the child was mine.
Those latticed fingers fanned his face
where startled eyes peeped through
like hope in hiding. Then he looked away
and hugged his father close. They spoke
but even as they did I caught his breath,
a moment's pain and then he lay there
cradled in my arms. My father wept,
his warm tears falling on us both, his smile

as radiant as the lake mist clearing.
How I loved him then, and how the echo
of those hoofbeats disappearing and that howl
of loss which filled the air around us
meant so little, although sometimes
when my love-child comes to me
and knows it's past his bedtime he will find me
weeping but must not know why.

Simpleton

They stopped him on his way to the fair
and asked impossible questions.
I don't know he answered, one by one,
but with a simple grin they might
find fetching. Not a bit of it. Their laughter
thundered overhead, a dark cloud
gathering impatience. Then there rained
such blows on him he knew for sure
he'd never get there. *We could tell you
everything,* they said, *but this is better
and was worth the wait.* At that
he lay face down and took it, weeping
earthwards. One by one
the stars came out, and then the moon
was there, by now too late
for anything but shining vacantly
on all of them. The road ahead
returned a distant music and the pulse
of love until whatever started this
was over. *Now if he doesn't know*
he heard them say, *he'll never,* as they
left him, as he rose and stood there
shrouded in the certainty of pain,
remembering the questions. Then
towards him, innocently decked
with ribbons from the fair, a girl
came dancing and she broke his heart.

Grandmother's Advice

Cry wolf.

*

Listen to the echo
as it gives away his name.

*

Be ready when he comes
for all eventualities.
There will be plenty.

*

Look suitably afraid,
a wolf expects it
as a prelude to the tenderness
he knows must follow.

*

Display the sweetmeats
in your basket, play
with him a little, tickle him
behind the ears, caress
his starveling flanks.

*

Ask him *Are you hungry?*,
knowing that he is,
then as his eyes light up
produce the apple,
take a bite yourself
and promise everything.

*

Remind him of his better nature,
walk with him into the wood
engaged in moral conversation
(he'll excel at this)
and ask if he first loved you
for your crisp intelligence
or for your scarlet hood.

*

Lead him to the cottage,
enter it together, ask
whatever happened to my story,
why the bed is empty,
do not trust his alibi,
his guilty look.

*

Back off, bolt the door
behind you, check
your basket, take no notice
of his howling when it fills
the forest with its pain.

*

Make for home
along a tidy path
which was not there
before.

*

Note with some surprise
that you are
disinclined to hurry.

*

Take one last bite
from the apple.

*

Throw away its core.

The Wolf-mask

Father, a wolf-mask comes after me
strapped to your dear face
which I loved for its gift of security
no cruel disguise could replace.

So why do you haunt me now
with a grin and a false red tongue
as if to say: *This is what I could not tell you*
when you were young –

as if you needed to hear me ask
for the truth after all this time,
to have me tear off your wolf-mask
and acknowledge it as mine?

Going Native: 1918

Father, listen, I have come to say
goodbye, to you, to all of this,
a life no longer life, the courtesies
which smiled and smiled
but could not turn a single hair
to save our Nation. Were you here
I think perhaps you'd understand
for once and not quote Shakespeare
though if you did I'd parry
There's a world elsewhere, a brave one
with such people in it
as we've never known. Enough
of King and Country, of the table
on a roar, good fellowship,
the joining of the ladies, trade
with those less fortunate, the rituals
we lived by. I have booked my passage
and I ask your blessing in this room
where last I came to see you
though you turned your back ...
These are the last words I shall speak
before I lose my tongue, become
the gossip of my legend, stuff
that everybody's dreams are made on
but which nobody believes.

So I have returned the silver
to its velvet, run a finger once more
round the frame which holds
your portrait, pinched the dust
and blown it mote and beam
to gather sunlight. Something exquisite
about departure, all those books
I'll have no need of, each a tempter
flourishing its gilded spine, a backbone

snapped there to attention. No,
no more of this; the parakeet
is shrieking in its cage, *farewell
the plumèd coop*, the lawn
pursues its trimmed declivities
by jingo to a swamp. What life is here
but little England's bulldog pugface
slumped on the parterre
to strains of Elgar? I shall put this
in a verse for you, for all of us,
and maybe I shall leave it by the inkstand,
maybe not. Whatever happens now
is off the map and needs no record
except this: The gentleman I was
bowed out according to your rules
because they would not serve. The rest
must be a darkness at the heart
of all I never dared to put a name to
or a shining river taken at the flood
and out of time. Whoever wonders
What became of him?, sets out
to join me there or bring back
my remains, will miss the point
and come home silent. So
to business. Father, all my papers
are in order. I have settled the estate
and laid your ghost. Our dust
will thread us both together for a last time
in this torque of sunlight
as I leave the room. The bearers
have arrived. I hear them.
Pray for me ...

The Rapture

(For Eamon Duffy)

The manic cat claws up its wall of glass,
all grin, where once a dumb dog
nodded. So the expected comes to pass –
Alpha and Omega, Gog and Magog

nose to tail along the highway
stepping on it westward. *Jesus,*
give me out! There's no abiding stay
for the fresh-packed kids on this bus.

Oh Lord, the hairs of each innocent head
are numbered, such a quantity
of love, the sum of it, a downy, tousled
congregation. The pity, Lord, the pity ...

So take me now amidst their laughter
as the dove descends, its wings
aflame with gasoline, become the rapture
of your servant risen beyond all things

locked here in this endlessness
of driving headlong nowhere
never to be born again. But bless
each child. It was trusted to my care.

His Dream

He told her:: 'I was on a platform, staring
at the blank face of my watch, no other
passenger in sight, and it was
somewhere I had been before
but couldn't name the station. In my palm
what seemed to be a silver coin was faceless too
but whether it was currency to pay
or small change not worth pocketing
I couldn't tell. No one had left me
with instructions, but I knew exactly
what must follow ...
                        'Always
it was just like this, becalmed
and purposeless, a cold light
shining on the rails which picked them out
from darkness. Then there would come
a shudder from the points, a hum,
a signal crashing down, and then
a distant, dull explosion. So the train
I knew must soon be passing through
drew nearer, and I knew
I could not be allowed to wake before it passed
and once again must witness every window
shattered, each compartment
packed with children sitting there
bolt-upright, gazing straight ahead,
with bright wax faces, little boxes
on their knees, peaked caps
and scarlet uniforms. I heard a tannoy
crackle as the carriages rolled by
but no voice spoke ...
                        'And then I'd turn around
to walk away, but every time
what seemed escape was darkened
by her shadow as it fell across my path

and wrapped around me weeping,
bitter with reproach, as if
she'd known I must have wished
the dream to come again
and meet me there without her
which was always when I woke
to find myself alone ... '

      'Not now,
not now,' she said, 'not any more,'
and made it sound so easy
as they lay together, as she took his hand
across the narrow space between them,
holding on until quite sure he was asleep.

The Loss

All winter something tightened its grip
which was not exactly cold or loneliness
but an icicle cry, a bright ring of distress,
a muffled sounding with pain at the tip.

It was not exactly what they had decided
either between them or by individual choice
left undiscussed. It was not a distinct voice
but a last-chance line which would not go dead.

Often they woke together in the early hours
to shift to back-to-back then sleep again,
never to give the accident its name
because the night was over and the loss was theirs.

She Won't Come to the Door

She won't come to the door

You can try the horse-shoe knocker
The chime's major third

She won't come to the door

You can trap your fingers in the letter-box
The brass knuckle-bruiser

She won't come to the door

You can print your shadow on the frosted glass
Your feet on the last step

She won't come to the door

It is nothing you have done
It is nothing you have said

She won't come to the door

You are no part of this
You are not in it

She won't come to the door

Not for the life
Not for the love

She won't come to the door

Last Look

He weighed so little. They carried him out
for a last look at the garden.
It blazed with autumn sunlight.
Gently they put down their burden.

Grief, not flesh, was the heaviness.
He asked to be left there.
'Troops, dismiss!'
A flash of the old order.

Nothing to do but obey.
The family mock salute.
At ease. Stand easy.
Go inside and wait.

So little. They watched from the house
for as long as it took
(which was hardest, they told us)
then carried him back.

The Windbreak

With the heat of a sand bed
Shifting under us, dry salt
on our lips, your slabbed hair
pressed to my face
in the first year of our marriage.

We had stepped from the ocean
together, lain down
deeper in love than land
knew how, or than
sun and air could make it.

Why should there not be
day after day like this, a lifetime's
hunger for our bodies'
weight of expectation
grateful to the end?

Then when it comes,
to step out from the windbreak's
arm around us, back
towards resolving water
and the source of love.

High Summer

Too hot to sleep even at midnight
with a little breeze now
and the streetlights off
we walk around the block, old-stagers
of romance, my warm hand
on your naked shoulder.

Others are out too
in this turn-about dissolve
to early morning, shadows
of themselves with
assignations burning
but beyond recall.

My hand slips down
to lace our fingers
while so much to come
is haunting here
between my footsteps
and the pattern on your dress.

The Couples

(For Mary)

It was trial by error
at the edge of the floor
as I watched them altogether
at ease with one another,

how he'd light a cigarette,
taking his time over it
and fill her empty glass
with a smile which said *Yes*,

how all I could think of
was what being in love
like that might do, and having
a girl of my choice to bring

then take the long way home
instead of this familiar cousin
they'd fixed me up with,
this sudden death

by expectation. *So
you can't dance then?* No.
Which was all there was to that.
We had to sit it out

in a pair of available
chairs, upright along the wall,
miserably side
by conspicuous side

while from each table,
couple by couple,
the floor was suddenly thronged
with the real thing

where he would whisper
the right words in her ear,
and she would say *Yes*
and again *Yes Yes*

as the lights went down,
as they went on and on,
as we said nothing to each other
as it seemed forever,

and even now I blush,
remembering that sly moustache,
waxed and pencil thin
above the bandleader's grin

though, later, your amused patience
when I first tried to dance
led to these thirty years of marriage
from the same floor's edge.

The Black Cat

This was the year
of the black cat
visiting our garden
with its blood-red collar
and a silent bell.

We had not expected
its delayed arrival
or such witness
to the loss of friends.

What could we do
but bend to stroke it,
once for luck
and then again
to send it on its way?

When it returns
we'll not mistake
the look of recognition
in those distant eyes.

True Colours

Hosing at last light, and wondering
just how domestic he can get
and knowing all too well the price
of what he settled for and
doubting what may come of it beyond
such happiness as this, he notes
the glow of incandescence
on each leaf, and blue
more blue than ever, lemon
gold and carmine,
with the full moon waiting
for his change of heart.

Self Portrait in Middle Age

To have been the child of vicarage gardens
in a declining west, my hand-me-down
shorts and sandals from the Desert Rats.

To have sung *The Bells of St. Mary's* with my
Baptist aunt as a party-piece, while spaniels
flopped their cloth ears on the hearth-rug.

To have gone away to school, my initials
stencilled on a tuck-box, continuity
of status, little master, quid pro quo.

To have gowned it in cloisters, chained
a bicycle to railings, fixed my fool's head
for a season on the pole of lust.

To have come back less a stranger
than my vanished life's accomplice, homeless
at home, unready to move on.

To have ended misalliance, loving double
in a city bed, the pampered country boy
who slept away from mother.

To have hitched a ride with fortune,
picked up two bright children,
learned a different language over thirty years.

To have blessed each fresh arrival
at the point of waking, with that same
firm warmth beside me, glowing into age.

To have stared and stared back at the mirror
unbelieving, day by day, that luck
still holds and wears a lover's face.

For Better or Worse

LIFE ON A POGO-STICK

Suddenly into her life he came bouncing
with assets and equities called to account
and his charming assurance a column of figures
that leapt on the spot like a tall story
of everything high in the air and so giddy
that just to look up at him upset her balance.

Then suddenly too on the morning it ended
his head left the pillow and shot into orbit
already too far for a blown kiss to reach it
announcing no less than their flight from each other
and only the amorous bed of forsythia
sprang into blossom to bid them good-bye.

A SONG OF GREEN WILLOW

She sat down and wept but her mind was elsewhere
like a long-legged fly on the waters of Babylon
testing her grief for its deep possibilities
even though no one could guess from the surface
that only last night she had been with Prometheus
stealing the fire which she hoped would prove heavenly.

Sure of his love and divinely inspired
she had let down her hair like a song of green willow
mistaking this eloquent long-legged bastard
for all that an angel could possibly wish for
until she woke up to the fact he'd already
moved in on her silence and got what she wanted.

BRIEF ENCOUNTER

He wanted to show her the tomb of Karl Marx
so she waited for him at the wrought-iron gateway
in boots and a great-coat because it was snowing
on ground so well-soaked that the snow couldn't settle
then when he turned up they went in together
his hat sitting snugly beneath his umbrella.

When they found the old maestro she started to giggle
(which did not suggest an appropriate reverence)
because with a levity hard to ignore
on the solemn stone head sat a little snow hummock
as if it had blown in (she said) from Siberia
making the day although he hardly thought so.

THE GOOD HUSBAND

She always invented the dreams she told him
and wished that she didn't but there it was
since the break of his day was to wake to explain them
bolt-upright in bed like a Viennese doctor
which started her giggling under the duvet
then brought him back down to her into her warmth.

She loved him because he was quaint and reliable
such a fine husband she counted her blessings
and hadn't he always been good with the children
explaining their dreams at the family breakfast
which started them giggling over the cornflakes
until he felt sure they'd begun to invent them.

THE TANGLED WEB

When for the rhyme's sake he sat down beside her
the yarn that he spun was a dew-threaded filigree
catching the light like the lace of a wedding dress
not the meringue of her overnight negligee
worn for a promise she couldn't remember
though neither could he from the way he was talking.

Then slowly the dayglow turned false as it dawned on her
this was a net she would never be caught in
so tangled so knotted that all she could think of
was how the bed looked like a crate of bananas
hauled from the hold to the harbour of Afterwards
scaring her off with his legs crawling out of it.

TABLE MANNERS

Taught from the start that a good host made certain
that nobody ever had nothing to talk about
each of them worked at the grammar of dinner guests
season by season revised and updated
a chattering syntax of smart suits and dresses
which fashioned their dialogue over the table

where all that was said went in search of its speech-marks
or skipped from parenthesis into lacuna
to wait for such silence as doubled the interest
in stock where the least of investments was golden
while learning the relative value of language
their children spoke only when properly spoken to.

HOMES AND GARDENS

She hardly knew what there was left to miss out on
so bounded she was in a Tupperware nutshell
that thought of the dread of tomorrow seemed infinite
promising coffee and Viennese wafers
and faces outfacing the face she prepared
like a bay-window view of an offshore horizon.

So all that seemed left was the six o'clock shadow
the purr of his engine and tyres on the gravel
so leisured and stately she screamed with impatience
for nothing by now she could quite put a name to
but knew that it wasn't the prospect of amber
the chiming of cubes or the sight of his feet up.

The Mobile Rag

Out of your pocket, up to your face,
any occasion, any old place,
dial those digits, watch this space
doing the mobile,
it's in the bag,
yes, doing the mobile rag.

Chase your client, hurry that lunch,
bend your ear, let your shoulder hunch,
hear those Japanese numbers crunch
doing the mobile,
Porsch or Jag,
yes, doing the mobile rag.

Stride down the platform, turn on your heel,
swagger and strut from deal to deal,
small cogs know that you're the big wheel
doing the mobile,
light up a fag,
yes, doing the mobile rag.

Put in the boot, sharpen the knife,
this is the action, this is the life,
always cut short the call from your wife
doing the mobile,
nag nag nag
doing the mobile rag.

Honour your partner? Keep your old car?
Who the hell do they think you are!
Look at that split skirt over by the bar
doing the mobile,
good for a shag,
doing the mobile rag.

Wire up the e-mail, tighten the net,
shaft your department without regret,
there's room at the top and you'll make it yet
doing the mobile,
doing the mobile,
doing that mobile rag.

Fats

(For John Lucas)

Hammer those spatulate
ringed fingers, run

the vertiginous keyboard's
length, a thumbnail

gliss, then chase
the accident, the chancy

modulation, grin
at each gain revealed

by loss, throw back
that massive head, become

pure joy, the love-struck
face of it, a kid again

to pump your pedal car
along its track of sound

while all the others step aside
to send you round the block,

then home in triumph
to the here, the now,

the leap to your applause
in bulk made nimble by the light

of music, in the shimmy
of your outsize suit,

and mercy, mercy
where did you get those shoes?

Walking

(in mem. Bruce Turner)

Rim-shots and the beat's
continuum of now

to now, already
lost in time but making

up for it, the accident
accentuated, seized

to chance a sudden
path, propulsion

of the moment
towards choice, its hum

and counter point
like walking, feet firm,

into light, the going
well, the glance

which shares it
passed between you:

This is good and
when it comes again will

not surprise us
less than now.

Wild Bill

Not for him, the tremulous
vibrato of age, lip gone
or the bought-in teeth
on an instalment plan.
This is the furious
Fuck you, death
in the full face of it.
This is my man.

Wild Bill, all in his name
he stands here, hot
and ready. One by one
the boys step up
to claim their solo spot,
rehearsed, well-amplified.
A brisk shrug
as they move aside.

At last, the triple-fingered
loosening of valves,
arms up and out, he
glares at the microphone,
twists it the other way
then with a flat-
down stamp of his foot
begins to play.

Noir

(For Ben)

There was once a way
of walking from the night
and taking off your hat
before you noticed her,

of tapping out one cigarette
then offering another
in the camaraderie
of loneliness and sex.

It played a song
you both remembered
emptying one glass
and then another

while the barman
bunched his cloth
to make a mirror
where you sat.

It took your hat
to set it at an angle
with the cock-eyed optimism
of an easy rhyme

and she was easy too
like any other, or a way
of walking back into the night
for all things possible.

The Song of Harry Houdini

Upside-down in a water tank –
Mother, for this I have you to thank.

Vertiginous plunge with a rush of air,
manacled limbs and tentacle hair.

Face like a lost boy's, nose against glass
on a rainy day in the bottom class.

Look at me, love me, let me out.
I am all yours as I thrash about.

Mine is the terror that holds your breath,
shaman, showman, trickster of death.

Why did you leave me? Where have you gone?
Hear them applaud your drowning son

who suddenly breaks the waters, free –
genius, genie, miraculously

to leap from his bottle, streaming wet.
Love of my life, I shall reach you yet.

When Tommy Cooper Died on Stage

All he'd ever had to do was stand up there
with that pillar-box grin, gauche heavyweight
of legerdemain, his manic stare
a bewildered glaze, his two left feet
tripping the boards, so that when he died
it seemed the perfection of his act
in exquisite slow-motion, a long slide
into himself, such absolute control, the exact
moment recognised for what it offered
as the risk to take, a chance to bow out
on the wave of the applause he heard
from stalls and balcony, ignore the shout
of panic in the wings, his last breath
taken just like that. It was a poet's death.

His Walking Sticks

Whatever the day, wherever he went
they were the business when he took them out,
accessory to each sartorial variant
and syncopation in the dash he cut.

Lad-about town, his dandy swagger
spun to the tap of a pavement stone
or strode in tweeds through weekend heather
like Harry Lauder on his gramophone.

Such a variety of walking, style
for all occasions, absolute Englishness
defined by stepping out, no finical
remote concerns of nationhood or class.

Not even death could stop him in his tracks
until his family arranged today
to add them to the past that clearance takes
and watch an unhoused spectre limp away

Rushing Water

Every afternoon it seemed for ever
that we walked there
holding hands, my mother
naming it from my perspective
as the modest tumble grew
to roaring in my ears. It had to be
our best adventure, casting twigs
to speed along what made a mill-race
of a stream, to snag and tangle
in the overhang of grass then
break away and drift on
out of sight. Or sometimes
I'd have brought a paper boat
prepared (she'd say) *for all eventualities,*
a phrase which heralded
the soak to saturation
as its crew went down. For both of us
this was the current of our love
made dangerous, yet not to be
diverted from a sacred place.

When I ask if she remembers it
she'll only say *So much has happened.*
If you're sure then I suppose we did
but there's enough to think of.
Close the curtains, dear, the light
is shining in my face, I want
to look at you, to see me sitting
in my father's chair, once more
to call me by his name, to check herself
and mutter *What a muddle,* lift
the telephone receiver, sigh,
replace it, fumble in a drawer
for my last letter – *I forget*
if you don't write it down – repeat

again again the same the same
So much you're up to it's a wonder
you keep going... , nod
and fall to silence, leaving me
alone with just the two of us
arrived at Rushing Water, holding hands
across a flood become unbridgeable
in which I drown for love of her
as she lets go but cannot call my name.

After Clearance

This was the house in full possession
when from room to room
I drifted, saying goodbye to everything.

Goodbye bookcase, goodbye piano
in a grand style, connoisseur of self-pity
like Gayev in *The Cherry Orchard*.

Goodbye, even, to a leaf from the privet
held in my palm and then blown from it
or a watering-can in the greenhouse.

No good now at this last parting
to play again that little gentleman, pretend
my trunk is packed for setting off to school,

indulge an exquisite deprivation,
whisper *See you all at Christmas*
to a bedroom cupboard stacked with toys.

Not now. My mother dead, the chair
she sat in tottering on a skip
and all but one key with the agent.

Nothing left except to leave,
become historic, say Goodbye
reflexively from habit, check the lock

then drive away, a child
grown apprehensive for his wife and children,
all of us like privet in the palm,

the blinking of an eye.

The Promise

After five months
I meet her in a dream
with all the pain forgotten,
with the swelling in her legs
gone down, just back
from driving into town
and laden happily
with groceries. She says
Let's see about them later
as we run together
out into the garden as it was
in the beginning, where
an empty seat still swinging
waits on his perfected lawn,
unrusted, primal
in its lick of paint,
then there she is
before I know it, laughing,
Push me, push me harder,
oh if he could see us
but we'll tell him won't we
when we get there?
and her young face radiant
with expectation, and myself
once more the child seized suddenly
and held there in her lap
until whichever of us wakes
to keep the promise
offered by a dream.

The Waterfall

(For Brian Waltham)

Walk in deeper, hear the waterfall before you meet it
but without a thought of drowning, then look up
at all those rainbow colours leaping overhead,
the spectral drench of them. Lie back, become
your own horizon, let the flood plunge as it must
and watch your little house go bobbing home
to safety. Nothing you can do will alter this, not all
that calling after you from ship-shape windows
and the children waving. If the risk you took
is now your element be free in it, begin
the braving of new surfaces, the going under
and the casting up on land you never dreamed of
but which now seems destination. Climb there
through the veil, the arch of foam, until
it too becomes an echo left behind, a pulse
of comfortable love you all once danced to
in the garden. Then, laid out before you, find
the wilderness you chose, its lonely creatures
raging to be named, the loping beasts, fierce eyes
embedded in the shadow of a wing, perhaps
a single tree just coming into leaf, to do there
what you must. And in the end if you should tell me
as you will that this is rhetoric, an utterance
too empty and outmoded for the world we live in,
I shall try again to find a fresh way through it
with a different language, hear the waterfall
but in my own translation, throwing caution to the winds
that still might offer me the gift of danger
in this only lifetime, leaping free.

Now

Here with the sun behind me
I am twice my length and dancing
like a dog that bounds ahead
towards bright water.

Far enough gone
beyond reflection,
out of my depth at last
and not too late.

I have stepped for fifty years
so carefully on a shadow
that this sudden light
could yet make off with me.